MW01609198

Look Through The Leaves

Poems Inspired By
The Irish Landscape

By Cynthia Dite Sirni

Copyright © 2018 by Cynthia Dite Sirni

All rights reserved.
No part of this book may be reproduced
or used in any manner
without written permission of
the copyright owner except for the use of
quotations in a book review.
For more information, address:
www.cynthiaditesirni.com

In thanks to God,
and
for once and for always,
for Michael

"Neglect not the gift that is in thee."
1 Timothy 4:14

The Second Sight is rendered
to those who have the Gift—
The smoky fog of Inishmore
reveals them in the mist
Much in the way Damascus
shed the scales upon Paul's eyes —
If you look out from the cliff sides
you can see the Day Light rise.
She spins her dizzy entourage
and washes up ashore—
To choose the one who has The Sight
and the tongue to share the lore
While the phantoms of Before the Times
tinge the island all a gray—
It's the magic of the wisty wind
That shares the gift of
what to Say.

I wrote a Poem for the world
Upon my paper page-
and yet it was not spoken there
upon Killarney's stage.

Instead they bursted into song
bright children dancing with their feet
the pride of generations
keeping time within their seats.

The old men didn't come outside
They stayed inside the pub
Like the chairs they sat upon;
worn and strong and loved.

I hid within the shadows-
The day not yet defined
When I spotted Mother Nature
With her posture from behind.

So I sat and watched the Day break-
The son of Mother Earth
She swaddled him in purple flannel,
Still pale from giving birth.

Her yellow sleeves embraced him
And brought him to her breast—
His tiny head was pinkly peeking
as he stirred from Rest.

He nuzzled on her shoulder
A Sun so blessed with brawn,
Held up his head to look at me —
And with a yawn,

He dawned.

A herd of apparitions
were startled by the dawn—

They vaporized in front of me
as I recognized a fawn

As still as I could hold myself
I watched them with my eyes—

As they stared back and —
Turned Away-
Tails bouncing with Surprise.

Revelation

The moon is a peephole—
and I'm inclined

to peer inside….

So I can see—
Who's watching me.

An infiltrating March
it makes—

The snow upon the skies—
Insidious and hypnotizing
Where the tulip lies—

Each snowflake is a Universe
unleashed upon the Earth—

It spins its dizzy spell
upon

The Spring still
Giving Birth.

11

Suspended

Bee—

Loiters

and

Hovers

Staring

at

Me.

Muckross Abbey

The soul so well within the guarded walls
Recedes her secret self from all but me
The echoes of her past make subtle calls
The ghost of hoof marks etched for all to see.

The tower leans to stretch her mighty spine —
She rests upon the hills with sloping arms
A regal dame with brooding light refined
The sun flirts with the steeple and her charms

A languid silent lane she beckons forth—
A mass of shadowed chills within the heat
The finches shelter secrets for the court
of when the two of soul and heart will meet.

Did Oscar Wilde whisper
as I stood where he reclined?

I decided I was batty
so I continued on my stride

When I looked again and saw him lounging in
his perch —
I could have sworn I saw a twitch within that
famous smirk

I made a wish in Merrion Square
As bold as I, a mortal, would dare.
I couldn't help but hope that he
had really said these things to me

"…..and so The Day will slowly turn to Dusk —
The Light of Moon will Glisten
with the seas
A change within brings out an
Inner hush
More real than all the Dreams."

Lady Earth has an indigo shawl
I've seen it once at Dawn—

She wears it with an orange rouge
When suitors come to call.

She wears a fleeting perfume—
To match her floral dresses—

Shocks of waves and molten curves
Surround her yellow tresses.

The Mountainside's her posture—
A lounging silhouette—
She blows her windy kisses
as an Empty Covenant.

I thought I heard a Poem
As it rattled through the trees

I wasn't sure that she was there,
until She whispered to the Leaves

There was something to her voice
of ambiguity—
That heightened still within my soul
my sensitivity

When she saw me— she started out
And turned her head away

I knew it was the Sunrise in the
Trailing Wake of Day.

The raindrop doesn't waver,
falling from the sky

The bumble bee will hover
on the wind within the rye

The rainbow tangles ribbons
up within the misty tree—

How can all this Majesty
be waiting here for me?

The Silence of the Sunrise
whispers within my room—
Calling me to meet outside
of my contented womb.

I can smell the quiet city
still wet from all the rain —
It's the moment before Dublin wakes
And the chaos starts again.

Ode to The Summer Solstice

Within the dizzying dance she may—
pause to linger for this Longest Day,

Stretch herself within the skies
and Lead the Early Sun to rise.

Robed in a mist of azure blue,
She leaves behind a wake

Of Summer's children carrying her train,
And clinging for her sake,

To safely guide them into Light,
And bring them Lasting Glow—

The Longest Day throughout the Year—
Leaves Summer in her Tow.

Raising up her spirit here
within the shadowed mist—

A Quiet wraps within Itself
and Silence can't resist,

To saunter through the whispered trees—
And march between the mums....

The moment of the Darkness right before the
Morning Comes.

Nature's Benediction

The Earth became my altar—
The Mountains were a stair,

The birds of congregation
serenaded everywhere.

The Sun became communion host,
Offered to Most High.

The priests were Trees of Royalty
Their Sanctuary was the sky.

I genuflect at Sunrise,
and bless myself with Dew,

God's greatest gift of Morning
as life begins anew.

Autumnal Tree in Cashel

Like a Woman of a Certain Age,
she never hides her face —

Her color comes from deep within
her brilliance is her grace.

She keeps her arms up in the air —
head gurgling in laughter,

Strong and solid to see so fair
A woman to chase after

Her wisdom is a wake of truth
Her confidence is set —

She leaves a trail of glancing eyes
a life with no regret.

Silence, then was broken
by the Music of the Land—

A whisper through the dusky trees,
The Daybreak was at hand.

The gently lilting raindrops
Etch a pattern on the earth—

Each one profoundly different,
Who can estimate their worth?

The stirring of an angel's wings—
A special kind of grace—

A wind of hopefulness it brings
as it melts upon my face.

Through the window in Bushmills

The trees appear to shiver
As they adorn themselves with dew

They huddle like a mass of gulls —
A shade of whitened blue

They seem to have a message as they
Look inside at me....

But, what it is they try to say I
simply can not see.

Fairy Tree

The Leaves are birds of paper
Feathered in the tree
They hold their court above the earth
for all the world to see.

The sun acts as their jester
and tickles them with Heat—
Entwined within a nest
Her children sleeping at her feet.

Sonnet of The Trees

The trees appear to hide themselves within
Their pewter branches cased between the stalls
It seems as if their lives had died therein
The silence of the winter whisper calls

It beckons them to mull their inner muse
And nurture Spring who waits behind the plush
A wanton Miss whose touch does not refuse
The warmth of Sun awakened can not rush

A silent sense of softness seeps inside
The melody that flows will stir the trees
A change begins to spawn a Spring Denied
Her youthful blush will cling unto the leaves

A filmy shawl she wraps around her trunk
And waits for suitors of the Spring Defunct.

To see the night ubiquitous
with eyes left open wide
The stars create continuous
ripples mimicking the tide.

The Moon is just a wafer,
Her feet swinging in the Sea
I cannot tell quite where she ends
— until she winks at me.

The final flickered flares of Day
have tamped out underfoot
The ocean woven to the Sky —
The waves as dark as soot.

If it wasn't for the silence
I could have heard the Sky—
but the void of night was vast and loud —
I didn't hear her say goodbye.

There was a tiny Morsel
of the Universe alone—
She seemed to be enjoying it,
Single, Solitary, Stone.

The shadow left within her wake
was a continuation,
Her solidness and girth in hand
was an annunciation.

A tiny piece of history
That men had held between
their hands throughout the ages
Of what Her eyes had seen.

To weather on through epochs
and be part of Mother Earth
to see the eons lining up
as Time keeps giving birth.

Solitude is Someone
who will take you by surprise —
You didn't know
you were seeking her
until she looked you in the eyes,
Recognition takes an instant
and
reunion feels so sweet—

Your breath recovers differently
and
You feel your spirit heat —
A momentary lapse of Day
of time spent
All alone
A reservoir that fills again
in silence all your own.

Ode to Boding

Screaming Winds of Wild Women
echo high above the cliffs.
Sfumato fog and heavy clouds
shroud the ocean in the mist,

A hollow, barren emptiness
that fills the air with salt—
The Gray Lady wears her regal robes
as she continues on her walk,

Her train— it drags itself
along the jutted shore,
It wipes away the smoky sand
and makes the waters roar.

Incessant is her wailing
as she drapes herself in grief —
As she remembers all the sailors
who've been lost along the reef

The women folk still fear her,
They're afraid to raise her ire—
And they pray the winds will settle
and let their fishermen retire—

They count the time on rosaries
and weep without a sound
and pray that if the boat is lost
that their husbands will be found.

The sun is playing moody —
He turns his face both east and west
And tosses all the little boats
through shards of rolling crests

And the moments last forever,
and a split second is too fast
while the men folk are out fishing
and their heads keep looking past —

To see the green horizon
as it rushes out to meet them,
another day of safe return
their family waits to greet them.

A flock of stars suspended still
Above the crown of trees —
The wind breaks through the silent night
and moves them through the leaves

The shimmer bounces off the night
It whispers to the lichen —
It makes such noise for when it does
I can not hear the quiet.

The poet sees a natural muse
above a Canopy of Dreams—
They house the second sight of image
And know what the secret means

A hopeful thread against her breast—
She fingers at the twine
Commands a sage, elusive thought
to Yield into her mind

A nest begins to build itself
To lure a fragile bird
To perch within the circle
To become the Perfect word.

The way the birds can congregate
A flipping head of hair—
The movement can perpetuate
A single leaf blown through the air

They follow notes of symphony
And scale the notes like trees—
They move as one illustrious sheet
as a battalion of the bees

Kaleidoscope together
wave a flag of Art precision—
Which one among them is their leader
Who makes the group's decisions?

They synchronize their beating wings
And hop aboard the draft
Resembling a filigree of twigs,
That crest against a raft—

They hear a silent song within
To which they all respond
Until they huddle down together
At the hemline of a pond.

34

Ode to the Grave of W.B. Yeats

Benbulbin guards the tomb of Yeats
He stands at full attention—
It seems the least that he could do
since Yeats always gave Him mention —

The County Sligo's favorite son
Lay sleeping near the door —
Of the little church that housed his
"Granda" there many years before

His resting place is a Poem —
It's appropriate and fine
For a man who conjured words
That continue for all Time.

Gap of Dunloe

Through the cleavage of her bosom
is a reflection of the sky—
The purple sheep are loitering
between the pebbly birds that fly.
The wild horses are a river's bend
who wander as they graze—
If you move up silently,
They'll stare right into your face.

Although they do not speak a word
They have the Second Sight, y'know.
You can see it in their wisdom
in the way they watch you go.
Although they will not tell us
as the hills render them mute,
They convey an offering of peace
That the Silence can't refute.

If your feet are on the Wishing Bridge
and you spot a Fairy Tree —
You'll be sure the Gap is smiling
down upon the Little Twee.

The Fishermen of The Castle Ross
Hold court under the tree
My favorite one stays to himself —
A blinded dog sits at his knee.

He doesn't need to speak at all
The dog knows what he's thinking—
they guard each other from the rest
and spend the day both blinking—
looking towards the water's side,
away from ducks and carriage rides.

The tourists wait to meet him
as they're standing on the slip
The dog is frozen in his spot—
both blind and with bad hips.
He opens up his arms splayed wide
The dog licks his rugged face—
He smiles as they climb aboard
reposed in an Embrace

The others may be snickering
near the rowboat mausoleum
But neither man nor dog will care
if anyone can see 'em.

A Rainbow climbed up on us
as we sat along the shore—
We could see the Swans of Galway
and the boats from Inishmore

She didn't want to scare us
She approached us in a hush
but we already saw her there—
She made the day light blush

She flirted with us fully
Perched demurely on the bog wood
and then she shook herself of water
much in the way a dog would—

Although it started raining
as she left us in her wake —
The sun continued playing
splashing water in the lake.

Kilkenny

Over long across the way,
with the river at your feet
a sign appears that's saying
"Fresh Grocery, Stout and Peet"

Inside you'll find a grocery
with nothing that you need,
but you find that you must buy it all
because everything's so twee

The bar keep is the owner,
He's a good man through and through
he builds the Guinness and chews the fat
so proud to share the hurling stats

As Limerick won the shouts rang out
throughout the charming hamlet
Says he, "A 45-year drought has ended.
It's brilliant here now, damn it."

As the sun set on the Abbey
and the stained glass gleamed its light
The castle looked down at the village
so as to memorize the sight.

It means —
Wild Atlantic Way
a nondescript small sign
a copper plate with
WAW
leads you on the line
As you balance on the cliff tops
and you battle with the roar
You cannot help but weep a bit
to see such beauty on the shore

Landscapes change from black and white
to colors beyond words
If you look closely you can see
"The Dolphin" flirting with the birds

The grasses flip their hair
like maidens at a dance
the ancient stone huts standing Still
barely giving you a glance

As far as the island's finger reaches
you can almost feel the need
To touch the Boston harbor
where she sits across the sea.

33703080R00024

Made in the USA
Middletown, DE
17 January 2019